First and Second editions published in The United States by **Holland Brown Books, LLC** 2010
Third printing published in The United States by the **Pierce Investment Company**, 2013

For more information contact Matthew Parker (matparker@gmail.com) or Vadis Turner (info@vadisturner.com)

ISBN 13: 978-0-9797006-7-5
ISBN 10: 0-9797006-7-1
Library of Congress Control Number: 2010913376

Nashville Counts! A Children's Counting & Art Book
2nd Edition

Written by Vadis Turner and Matthew Parker
Introduction by Ann Patchett
Edited by Stephanie Brothers

Contributing Artists:
Andy Perez, John Dunkerley, Lesley Patterson Marx, Jim Sherraden/Hatch Show Print®,
Kelly Williams, Trevor Mikula, Alan LeQuire, JPresley, Bryce McCloud, Langford Barksdale,
Vadis Turner, Lauren Rolwing, Herb Williams, Samuel Dunson, Matt Reasor, Polly Cook,
Myles Maillie, William Edmondson, Rosie Paschall, Wayne Brezinka, and Emily Leonard.

Supplementary Photography by John Guider
Graphic Design by Ty Kreft
Cover Illustration by Amanda Bishop

Typeset and Printed in Canada.

Manufactured by Friesens Corporation in Altona, MB, Canada
March 2013

Job # 82296

NASHVILLE COUNTS!

A COUNTING & ART BOOK

written by Vadis Turner and Matthew Parker
introduction by Ann Patchett
edited by Stephanie Brothers

With generous contributions from 21 Nashville Artists...

Andy Perez, John Dunkerley, Lesley Patterson Marx, Jim Sherraden/Hatch Show Print®, Kelly Williams, Trevor Mikula, Alan LeQuire, JPresley, Bryce McCloud, Langford Barksdale, Vadis Turner, Lauren Rolwing, Herb Williams, Samuel Dunson, Matt Reasor, Polly Cook, Myles Maillie, William Edmondson, Rosie Paschall, Wayne Brezinka, and Emily Leonard.

supplementary photography by John Guider

THANKS

to everyone that played a part in the creation of Nashville Counts.

INTRODUCTION

by Ann Patchett

There are a lot of things in this world that are wonderful when they're dry, and completely worthless when submerged under water – think cakes and paintings. Then again some people, great swimmers for example, need water in order to shine. When Nashville was flooded in May of 2010, the city took it as an opportunity to shine. Neighbors helped neighbors bail out their basements, singers sang in benefits for flood relief, schools held bake sales, people invited strangers into their homes, and volunteers went out and did everything from scrubbing muddy floors to hauling away trash.

Sure, we would have preferred that the city hadn't flooded at all. Many people suffered and some of them are still struggling to get back on their feet. But the silver lining to this otherwise dark rain-cloud is that now Nashvillians know who our friends are. If there's trouble, we can count on just about everybody to lend a hand.

Even now you're helping flood victims by buying this book. And since we're counting on you to tell your friends about it, we feel like the least we could do in return is show you some great things around town that we like to count. On behalf of Nashville, we appreciate your support. Now that we're dry again, we hope you'll come visit.

There is **1** capitol in the state of Tennessee... and it's in Nashville!

2 U.S. presidents called Nashville their home: Andrew Jackson & James K. Polk.

The serpent's body at the Dragon Park has

3 arches. The third arch has a portrait of Fannie Mae Dees, a community activist who made the park possible.

The Grand Ole Opry is the most famous country music radio show in the world! Roy Acuff hosted the 4 hour live broadcast from the Ryman Auditorium.

Oprah Winfrey began her career on Channel 5 News. She was both the first female and first African American anchor in Nashville.

Elvis Presley's

solid gold Cadillac has **6** gold records attached to the ceiling! You can see it at the **Country Music Hall of Fame.**

The Parthenon was built for the World's Fair in 1897. The bronze doors weigh **7** tons each! Heavy enough to protect the goddess Athena inside.

There are 8 Colleges and Universities in Nashville: Belmont University, Fisk University, Lipscomb University, Meharry Medical College, Tennessee State University, Trevecca Nazarene University, Vanderbilt University, Watkins College of Art and Design.

Nashville's Union Station opened in 1900.

Can you count 9 trains?

There are 10 cellists in the Nashville Symphony Orchestra.

There are 11 Titans football players on the field during every play. Go Titans!

The Goo Goo was America's first candy bar. **12** Goo Goos make a dozen. One Goo Goo is on the Go Go.

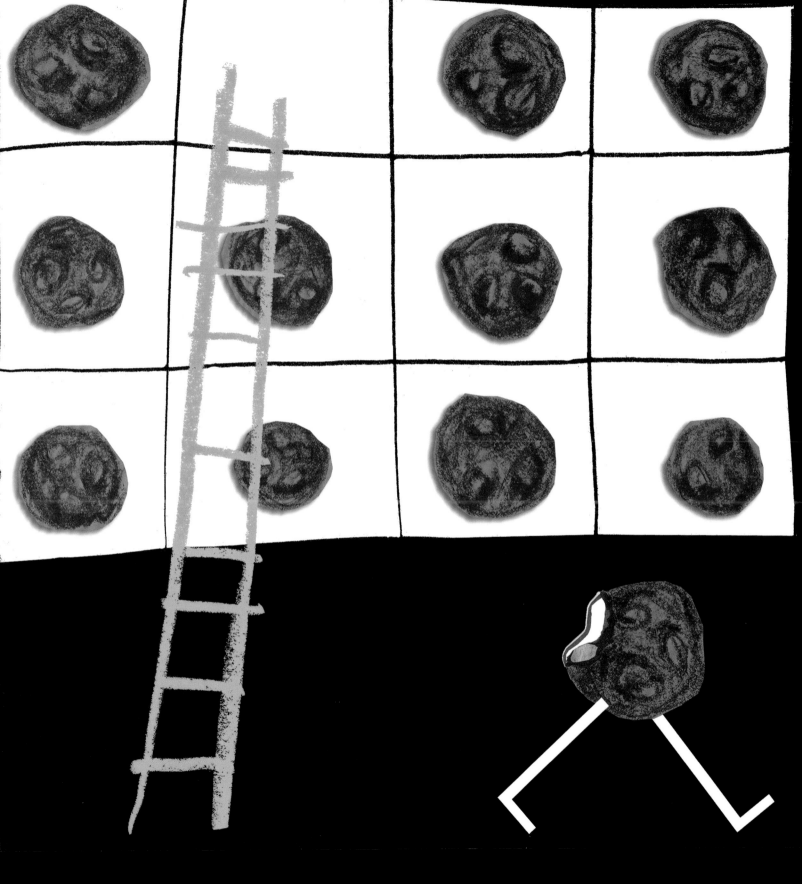

The Frist Center for the Visual Arts was originally a post office. The geometric designs in the architecture are typical of the the Art Deco style. Can you find triangles? 13

Nashville has the hottest chickens around. Can you find 14 chickens at the Hot Chicken Festival?

At the **Pancake Pantry,** you get silver **15** dollar pancakes in every stack!

There are **16** ounces in a pound of Maxwell House Coffee. When President Theodore Roosevelt tried it at the Maxwell House Hotel he said it was "Good 'til the last drop".

Nashville's Music Row starts at 17th Avenue South. Musicians from all over the world come to make records there.

Limestone is known as Tennessee Marble. It has been used to construct buildings since the 18th century. Nashville artist William Edmonson used it to make sculptures.

Take a trip back in time & cruise the Cumberland River on the Gen. Jackson, a replica of a 19th century riverboat.

Can you count **20** pink flamingos that live at the Nashville Zoo?

NASHVILLE ZOO

THE END.

Nashville Artists

Emily Leonard (intro)

In my work, I am always looking for something to unfold; to know again what I have known forever. My paintings are often of mornings and evenings. I am drawn to these moments when the trees are weary and sinking into their deepest roots, as if to remember where the seed came from. My process and my product begin to intersect as I draw on the experience of seeing, as an inroad to knowing. I paint to understand the story of the space between a viewer and an object, between the air and the land, between creator and created.

Andy Perez (1)

Andy Perez is an illustrator, artist and designer. Originally from Kentuckiana, he received a Bachelor of Fine Arts from The Milwaukee Institute of Art and Design, where he studied Illustration. Since then, Andy's work has been featured in publications and galleries across the United States. His work is primarily executed with collage and acrylic paint along with other mixed media. He currently resides in Nashville, TN with his beautiful wife and daughter.

www.andytheillustrator.com.

John Dunkerley (2)

John (Jed) Dunkerley, born and raised in Nashville, has called Seattle home for the last 14 years, where he is a high school art teacher, exhibiting painter, performance artist and illustrator. His art can be seen in Tennessee on the Jubilee Nut Brown Ale packaging, a collaboration with his brother Mark, Jubilee's founder.

Lesley Patterson Marx (3)

Lesley Patterson-Marx was born and raised in Louisville, KY and has lived in Nashville, TN since 2001. She received a BA in Fine Art from Murray State University in 1997 and an MFA from The University of North Carolina, Chapel Hill in 2001. Her favorite mediums to work in are printmaking, mixed media on paper, and book arts. In addition to exhibiting her work both locally and nationally, she works as a teacher and illustrator, having taught at Watkins College of Art and Design and University School of Nashville. She is proud to live with four Nashville natives; her husband, son, and two dogs.

www.lesleypattersonmarx.com

Jim Sherraden Hatch Show Print®(4)

Jim Sherraden is Manager, Chief Designer and Archivist at Hatch Show Print®, one of America's oldest surviving show poster and design shops. Since 1984 he has overseen its transition from a cultural survivor to a widely recognized graphic design icon and destination for letterpress enthusiasts. He is the co-writer of *Hatch Show Print®, The History of A Great American Poster Shop*, published by Chronicle Books, now in its fifth edition. He is also the creator of one-of-a-kind pieces of art called monoprints, based on the shop's archive, which are collected by individuals and institutions worldwide. He frequently speaks and conducts letterpress workshops from coast to coast.

Kelly Williams (5)

Kelly Williams is a Nashville native who has returned to her hometown after earning a BA from Vassar College and a MFA from the School of the Art Institute of Chicago. She works from home, in a spare room, often while listening to the tv or radio, and depicts images of familiar or curious domestic spaces in oil on canvas. Williams has served as an

Nashville Artists

adjunct professor at The University of Wisconsin-Milwaukee, SAIC and Watkins College. Williams has also been awarded painting residencies by Yale University, The Terra Foundation of American Art, and the Ora Lerman Charitable Trust.

www.kellyswilliams.com

Trevor Mikula (6)

Trevor Mikula works with a palette knife, vibrant paint and little regard for conservation. The results are beautiful pieces full of life. Trevor regularly exhibits at galleries across the country including Wilde Meyer Gallery in Scottsdale/Tucson, Bennett Galleries in Nashville and Austin Hill Art in Atlanta. He is in numerous private and corporate collections across the country. He resides in Nashville, TN.

Elvis' Cadillac appears courtesy of The Country Music Hall of Fame® and Museum

Alan Lequire (7)

Alan LeQuire is a figurative sculptor, well known for his public commissions and sensitive portraiture. LeQuire works in a variety of materials, including wood, stone, gypsum, and cast bronze. He has completed a number of architectural, collaborative and site-specific projects since he began

accepting commissions in 1981. Most notably are his Athena Parthenos, the largest freestanding interior statue in the Western world, and Musica, the largest bronze figure group in the United States.

JPresley (8)

JPresley is an award-winning watercolorist who is best known for his landscapes and architectural renderings. He studied art in Madrid, Spain and in New Orleans where he attended the prestigious John McCrady Art School. It was in New Orleans where he learned to master the use of water media under Mary McCrady. His works have been displayed at numerous galleries and in many private collections.

"How can that which helps create such beauty be responsible for so much destruction?"

Bryce McCloud (9)

Bryce McCloud is proud to have been born in Nashville and still be allowed to live in the same city. For over a decade he has been at the helm of the letterpress print shop, Isle of Printing. IOP is dedicated to using, promoting and teaching the tradition of letterpress printing –

whilst melding it with the astounding advances of modern technology. Bryce is dedicated to making the world a slightly better place through public art. It is his hope that hand carving and printing posters will positively impact his fellow man and lead eventually to the ability to travel through space and time. If you think making art for the street is a good idea or want to admire us at work – please visit the shop.

www.isleofprinting.com.

Langford Barksdale (10)

Langford Barksdale is a native of Nashville and has been an artist most of her life. She designed a poster for the Nashville Public Library and has her work in collections in Switzerland and North America. She received a BFA from the University of Georgia. Langford spent over a year as a resident artist in Northern California. Her work can be found in collections all over the globe, including Donna Summer's studio, Swiss L'Abri, Heritage Title and Mac Presents. She has led workshops for children at Cheekwood, the Aspen Art Museum, and the Anderson Ranch. For the past five years she has been living and working in Colorado.

www.langfordart.com

Nashville Artists

Vadis Turner (11)

Working with traditional craft materials and techniques, Vadis Turner has developed a visual language that traces the classification of heirlooms in a contemporary cultural context.

Vadis has exhibited all over the US and abroad. Her work is in the permanent collections of the Brooklyn Museum of Art, 21C Museum, Kentucky Museum of Art and Craft and the Egon Schiele Art Centrum.

Vadis was born in Nashville Tennessee. She received her BFA and MFA from Boston University. Vadis currently lives and works in Brooklyn, NY and is an Adjunct Professor at Pratt Institute.

Digital collage collaboration by Christine Jaeger

Lauren Rolwing (12)

Since Lauren Rolwing was a child, she demonstrated her creativity by creating many objects and little theatres. She attended Savannah College of Art and Design where she received a BFA in Illustration. She uses various techniques to produce her works: from the most traditional such as collage, gouache, watercolor, oil paints, acrylic paint, sewing, embroidery, to the more modern computer programs. She has received numerous international awards in the areas of poster design and children's book illustration. She is currently working as a freelance illustrator.

Herb Williams (13)

To most adults, the sight and smell of crayons produce specific memories of childhood. The twist in the road to nostalgia is the creation of a new object, from a medium in which it was not intended. This element of unexpected interaction and play had Herb at hello. Herb is one of the only individuals in the world with an account with Crayola. He creates sculptures out of individual crayons sometimes used in the hundreds of thousands. His sculptures have been exhibited internationally in museums, public arenas, hospitals, corporate lobbies and an Inaugural exhibit. Herb is represented by The Rymer Gallery in Nashville, TN, and The Rare Gallery in Chelsea, NYC.

Samuel Dunson (14)

Samuel Dunson was born and raised near Dayton, Ohio. He graduated with a BS in Studio Art from Tennessee State University in Nashville before completing his MFA in Painting at the Savannah College of Art and Design, in Savannah, Georgia. Samuel has worked for the past 10 years as a Professor of Art at Tennessee State University. He frequently exhibits locally and outside of Tennessee. Samuel's paintings and drawings are primarily concerned with introspective concepts. Although Samuel's work is primarily concerned with these personal themes, he composes them in such a way as to invite the viewer into his life without feeling voyeuristic.

Matt Reasor (15)

Matt Reasor is a Nashville native who has lived in New York and Los Angeles as an active member of the local visual arts, and music communities. In addition to paintin' n' craftin', Matt is a real estate agent, and songwriter. He currently resides in Nashville with his fiancé, and their affenpinscher Ben.

Polly Cook (16)

Polly Cook grew up in Nashville, and fell in love with clay taking pottery classes at the art center in Centennial Park when she was 10. She went on to get a BFA in ceramic and sculpture from the University of Tennessee, Knoxville. Her ceramics and paintings have been exhibited

Nashville Artists

Centennial Park when she was 10. She went on to get a BFA in ceramic and sculpture from the University of Tennessee, Knoxville. Her ceramics and paintings have been exhibited in galleries and art festivals across the country, and her work is included in many corporate collections. The art is narrative in nature, yet each piece suggests (rather than resolves) a story. Inspired by emotions, hope, desire, and longing, love is at the heart of all of her work.

Myles Maillie (17)

Myles Maillie's colorful and ubiquitous work adorns everything from buses and room size murals to t-shirts and ties, making him one of Nashville's most recognizable and enduring artists. Although his style is energetic, often full of frivolity, his work is nevertheless articulate and well conceived.

Myles' style continues to grow and his new pieces reflect the caliber and confidence of a well-seasoned and serious artist. At Studio East Nashville collectors and fans will find a wild assortment of Myles' fashionable ties and tees, along with highly crafted constructions and triptych paintings.

William Edmondson (18)

William Edmondson (1874-1951), the son of freed slaves, was born in rural Davidson County and moved to Nashville by 1890. At the age of 57, Edmondson began working with limestone using a hammer and a railroad spike. Edmondson carved for 17 years. He said, "I am just doing the Lord's work. I ain't got much style; God don't want much style, but He gives wisdom and sends you along."

William Edmondson stands among the most important self-taught artists of the past century.

Bess and Joe, c.1930s limestone. Cheekwood Museum of Art Purchase through the bequest of Anita Bevill McMichael Stallworth and gift from Salvatore J. Formosa, Sr., Mrs. Pete A. Formosa, Sr., Angelo Formosa, Jr. and Mrs. Rose M. Formosa Bromley in loving memory of Angelo Formosa, Sr., wife Mrs. Katharine St. Charles Formosa, and Pete A. Formosa, Sr. 1993.2.3

Rosie Paschall (19)

Rosie Paschall was born in England, educated in South Africa and trained as a surface and graphic designer. She worked in London in the sixties at Sandersons of London as a fabric and wallpaper designer, and at Liberty of London. She moved to Tennessee after marrying a Tennessee Rhodes Scholar and began her adventure into teaching in 1972. She is still teaching art at The Harpeth Hall School, despite the loss of her left extremities due to a stroke.

Wayne Brezinka (20)

As an illustrator and contributing artist, Brezinka has been commissioned by The Los Angeles Times, Neiman Marcus, The Johnny Cash family, The Washington Post and the Chicago Tribune. Wayne has also illustrated many ads, posters, music packaging, and consumer packaging, and is always looking for new venues for his work. His illustrations have appeared in Communication Arts, Print Magazine and most recently, the Society of Illustrators 52 show in New York. Through a unique combination of vintage and found ephemera, collage and mixed mediums, Brezinka creates and sculpts these items into unique images and works art. Wayne lives with his wife and three children in Nashville, Tennessee.